PEOPLE to KNOW TODAY

HILLARY CLINTON

A Life in Politics

Jeff Burlingame

Enslow Publishers, Inc.
40 Industrial Road
Box 398
Berkeley Heights, NJ 07922
USA

http://www.enslow.com

To Bill Lindstrom: For his help, guidance, and friendship

Library of Congress Cataloging-in-Publication Data

Burlingame, Jeff.
    Hillary Clinton : a life in politics / Jeff Burlingame.
        p. cm. — (People to know today)
        Summary: "A biography of former first lady Hillary Rodham Clinton"—Provided by
publisher.
        Includes bibliographical references and index.
        ISBN-13: 978-0-7660-2892-0
        ISBN-10: 0-7660-2892-5
        1. Clinton, Hillary Rodham—Juvenile literature. 2. Presidents' spouses—United
States—Biography—Juvenile literature. 3. Women legislators—United States—
Biography—Juvenile literature. 4. Legislators—United States—Biography—Juvenile
literature. 5. United States. Congress. Senate—Biography—Juvenile literature.
6. Presidential candidates—United States—Biography—Juvenile literature. I. Title.
        E887.C55B869 2008
        973.929092—dc22
        [B]   2007029380

To Our Readers: We have done our best to make sure all Internet addresses in this book were
active and appropriate when we went to press. However, the author and publisher have no
control over and assume no liability for the material available on those Internet sites or on
other Web sites they may link to. Any comments or suggestions can be sent by e-mail to
comments@enslow.com or to the address on the back cover.

Cover Illustration: AP/ Wide World Photos

Photos and Illustrations: AP/ Wide World Photos, pp. 1, 7, 19, 20, 27, 37, 44,
51, 53, 55, 61, 63, 67, 78, 81, 90, 95; Corbis Corporation, pp. 4, 24, 33, 39;
Defense Visual Information Center, pp. 84, 93; William J. Clinton Presidential
Library, pp. 14, 47, 69, 71, 74, 76.

CONTENTS

A young Hillary Rodham on the campus at Wellesley College in 1969.

1
A HISTORIC SPEECH

No one knew what to expect when it was Hillary Rodham's turn to speak. Wellesley College was almost one hundred years old, but no student had ever given a graduation speech. It almost did not happen this time, either. The school's president, Ruth Adams, had to think long and hard before finally allowing it. She wanted to know who the speaker would be. Rodham told her, "Well, they asked me to speak."[1]

It was no surprise the Class of 1969 had chosen the popular Rodham to be its speaker. In fact, no one else was considered. The college president later said, "There was no debate . . . as to who their spokesman was to be."[2] What she ended up saying made it a historic moment for many in her generation.

On graduation day, a dynamic United States senator spoke immediately before Rodham. He was the country's first-ever African-American senator, Edward Brooke. Senator Brooke talked about the sometimes-violent protests young people were staging across America. At the time, the country was dealing with many divisive issues, including a highly unpopular war in Vietnam. Many college students protested the war and other actions they did not believe in. They often focused their anger on the government.

Senator Brooke told the graduates that protests were hurting the country rather than helping it.[3] He said many of the protesters were doing so "without purpose."[4] He said it was "a perversion of democratic privilege."[5] He believed the United States would be better off if the protests stopped. The senator wanted everyone to stand behind the government.

While she waited her turn to speak, Rodham grew frustrated by the senator's comments. She and her classmates were among those he was talking about. But Rodham felt protesting was important for her generation. She believed all Americans should be allowed to voice their opinions whenever they felt like it. She also was upset that the senator did not speak about any of the issues she and her classmates were concerned about. Years later, Rodham said the senator had talked as if everything was fine in the world. She knew it was not.[6] Popular leaders, like Martin Luther King Jr., had recently been assassinated. America was fighting in an unpopular war. Minority groups, such as African-Americans and women, were vying for equal rights. In many ways, the country was in turmoil. But the senator did not mention any of those issues in detail.

Rodham stayed up most of the night before graduation nervously writing her speech. Several friends helped her and offered suggestions. But when she heard Senator Brooke's comments she decided to change her plans at the last minute. After the college president introduced her to the crowd as "cheerful, good humored, good company, and a good friend to all of us,"[7] the twenty-one-year-old Rodham stepped up to the microphone. She began with a response to the senator. Friends remember her speaking for ten minutes off the top of her head before finally beginning her prepared speech.[8]

When he had spoken, Senator Brooke mentioned that 13.3 percent of Americans were living below the poverty

Edward W. Brooke served as a Republican senator from Massachusetts from 1967 to 1979.

line. He said this to make a point that the country had improved. During her speech, Rodham asked, "How can we talk about percentages and trends?"[9] She felt each person living in poverty was a human being and should not be treated as a number by a politician trying to make the government look good. She said there should be "respect between people where you don't see people as percentage points. Where you don't manipulate people."[10] She also said every protest is important and politicians should be trying to make "what appears to be impossible, possible."[11] Her speech was full of passion.

The crowd's reaction to her speech was mixed. The older people were embarrassed and shocked that a young woman would speak that way, especially in front of and about a United States senator. A mother of one graduate said, "I would have liked to have stopped her. I'm sure her mother would've liked to have stopped her. But her class absolutely encouraged her. And when she finished, they rose in a body and applauded her."[12]

One of those four hundred cheering classmates remembered Rodham's fiery speech. She said, "It was brash, it was brilliant, it was unplanned and it was disrespectful to Senator Brooke.

. . . I can remember squirming in my seat. At the same time, the inner me was saying 'Alright!' "[13] Another classmate turned to her mother and said, "Take a good look at her. She will probably be the president of the United States someday."[14]

After the graduation ceremony, Rodham headed to a lake on campus. Swimming was not allowed, but she jumped in anyway. During the next few days, Rodham's speech became national news. Fighting for what she believed in—especially in opposition to a high-ranking politician—made an impact on her country. The graduation speech proved to be just the beginning for her. But at the end of an action-packed day in the spring of 1969, Hillary Rodham was not concerned with her future. All she wanted to do was go for a relaxing swim. So she did, on her terms.

2

YOUNG REPUBLICAN

Chicago had seen its share of major events by the time Hillary Diane Rodham was born there on October 26, 1947. The four red stars on the city's flag tell the story of Chicago's rich history. Two stars represent the two World's Fairs the city hosted. The fairs were visited by millions of people from across the world. One star stands for a bloody battle fought near the Chicago River during the War of 1812. The fourth star symbolizes a massive fire that swept through the lakeside metropolis in 1871. The blaze killed nearly three hundred people and wiped out miles of houses, roads, and shops. It was called The Great Fire and burned for nearly two days. The fire left about one hundred thousand of the city's three hundred thousand people homeless.[1]

The Great Fire also destroyed much of the grandeur Chicago's gritty residents had worked years to achieve. Its citizens were not defeated. Shortly after the fire, they turned their sorrow into inspiration. "Chicago" is an American Indian word meaning "strong" or "great,"[2] and its saddened residents were both. Following the fire, they rebuilt their city into one of the largest and most powerful in the United States. By 1900, 1.7 million people lived in Chicago.[3] When Hillary was born, 3.5 million people did.[4]

First-time parents Hugh and Dorothy Rodham were two of them. Hugh Rodham was a gruff thirty-six-year-old businessman from Pennsylvania. He was a former college football player and a Navy officer during World War II. When Hillary was born, he owned and operated a small drapery business called Rodrik Fabrics. The window of his office looked out across the Chicago River.

Like many women of her era, Dorothy Rodham was a homemaker. She was born Dorothy Howell twenty-eight years earlier in the same Illinois city in which she gave birth to Hillary. By that time, the new mother already had lived a tumultuous life. Her parents were young when she was born and quickly proved unable to take care of her. So, at age eight, Dorothy and her three-year-old sister were sent to a small town in California to live with their strict grandparents. At fourteen, Dorothy left her grandparents's home and moved in with a local family. She worked full-time taking care of the family's children. After she finished high school, Dorothy returned to Chicago. She met Hugh Rodham there after applying for a job at a company he worked for. The couple married in 1942.

Hillary spent her first years living with her parents in a one-bedroom apartment. By the time she was three, her parents had saved enough money to pay cash for a house in Park Ridge, an upper-middle-class suburb fifteen miles north of Chicago. The family's two-story brick house on Wisner Street eventually became home to two more Rodham children: Hugh Jr., who was born three years after Hillary, and Anthony, who was born seven years after his big sister.

Their children's well being was a big reason the Rodhams picked Park Ridge. The suburb was known for its excellent schools, and education was very important to the Rodhams. The lifestyle there was much different than it was in Chicago. Hillary said, "[Park Ridge] was white and middle-class, a place where women stayed home to raise children while men commuted to work in the Loop, eighteen miles away. Many of the fathers took the train, but my dad had to make sales calls on potential customers, so he drove the family car to work every day."[5] Vanity may have been another reason her father chose to drive. Hugh Rodham's shiny Cadillac was one of his most prized possessions. He loved to show it off every chance he got.

The family's new neighborhood was full of children,

including many boys. This helped Hillary learn to fight for what she wanted at an early age. Her mother said, "She was able to play with the boys and, yet, sort of earn their respect."[6] Occasionally that respect had to be earned physically. One day, Hillary came home crying after a neighbor girl beat her up. She did not receive any sympathy when she got there. Her mother used the opportunity to teach her a lesson. She sent her back out to fight the girl. Hillary did, and the bullying stopped.

Hillary's favorite childhood memories were the summer car trips her family took to her father's home state of Pennsylvania. Hillary's grandfather owned a cottage in the Pocono Mountains there. Hillary spent her days swimming in Lake Winola and exploring the tree-lined area surrounding the lake. Hillary said, "Those vacations were a big part of my childhood, not least because they provided some of the best times I ever had with my dad."[7]

Hillary was not only active during the summer, she was very involved year-round. She was a Brownie and, later, a Girl Scout, and was considered a tomboy. She enjoyed riding her bike, playing softball and kickball, and traveling with her parents to Chicago to watch Cubs baseball games at historic Wrigley Field.

To most of the Park Ridge families, religion was as important as recreation. The Rodhams attended the First United Methodist Church. Hugh Rodham, in particular, was a devout Christian. Hillary said he "prayed kneeling

The Rodham family (left to right): Hugh, Hillary, Hugh Jr., and Dorothy.

by the side of his bed every night."[8] Dorothy Rodham taught Sunday school at the church. Her three children were among her students.

Outside of church, Hugh Rodham was a gruff man and a strict father. He had high expectations for his children. He expected them to work hard, just as he did. He often taught them tough real-life lessons about what could happen if they did not. Hillary said he would drive the family "down to skid row to see what became of people who, as he saw it, lacked the self-discipline and motivation to keep their lives on track."[9] It is easy to understand why hard work was so important to Hillary's parents. Both had grown up during America's Great Depression, an era where money was scarce and jobs were hard to find. Families had to conserve to survive. Living through that time affected people's behavior long after the Depression ended in 1941.

The Rodham children were taught the value of hard work by being made to do it. The family was surviving just fine, but the children still were not handed what they wanted. "My parents gave me my belief in working hard, doing well in school and not being limited by the fact that I was a little girl," Hillary said.[10] "It really was the classic parenting situation, where the mother is the encourager and helper, and the father brings news from the outside world."[11]

Meeting her parents's high education standards was no problem for studious Hillary. She had little trouble getting good grades. Yet her tough father always pushed her to do better. Once, when Hillary brought home a report card with straight A's from junior high school, her hard-to-please father told the happy student, "Well, Hillary, that must be an easy school you go to."[12] Hillary was disappointed at her father's reaction, but she later said words like that from her father inspired her to work even harder.

Hugh Rodham's political beliefs also impacted Hillary. She said her father was "an old-fashioned

Republican, who, until he met Bill Clinton, eagerly pulled the 'R' [Republican] lever in every voting booth he ever entered."[13]

Hillary became involved in politics at a young age. The 1960 presidential election hooked her. That year, a Democrat, John F. Kennedy, was elected president of the United States. A number of people felt illegal votes had helped Kennedy win. Hillary and a friend decided to help Republicans do something about it. The two thirteen-year-old girls hopped a bus from Park Ridge to downtown Chicago to visit addresses voters had listed on their registrations. They were checking to see if they actually lived where they said they did. Hillary said she was dropped off in a poor neighborhood and told to "knock on doors and ask people their names."[14] She discovered some of voters did not live at the addresses they had listed. That was illegal.

Hillary returned home and told her father what she had done. She thought he would be proud, because he was one of those who thought Kennedy had stolen the election. But Hugh Rodham was not proud. Instead, he was upset his teenage daughter had traveled to

Republicans and Democrats

The two major political parties in the United States today are the Republicans and the Democrats. Generally speaking, Republicans are pro-business and conservative, and support limited government involvement in certain economic areas. Democrats, on the other hand, generally draw support from the working classes and minorities. They believe the government should be involved in society and economy as much as necessary to fix whatever problems may exist.

Chicago without an adult. Hillary said, "He went nuts."[15]

That year, Hillary also got her first summer job. She worked for the Park Ridge Park District watching over a small playground near her house. Hillary said, "I pulled a wagon filled with balls, bats, jump ropes and other supplies back and forth. From that year on, I always had a summer job and often worked during the year."[16]

On May 5, 1961, astronaut Alan Shepard became the first American to travel into space. Many Americans were inspired by the man's courage to do something only one other person had done. Hillary was inspired, too. She wrote to the National Aeronautics and Space Administration (NASA) saying she, too, would like to be an astronaut. NASA's response was not very encouraging. The agency wrote back and said it did not accept girls into its space program. Hillary was devastated. She said, "It had never crossed my mind up until that point that there might be doors closed to me simply because I was a girl."[17] Today, many women hold important positions. They are doctors, lawyers, presidents of large companies, astronauts, and almost everything in between. It is easy to forget there was a time when women were not allowed to do many things men did. In the early 1900s, for example, women were not even allowed to vote for the president of the United States. So NASA's reply, though it seemed harsh, was not unusual for the time. But that did not make Hillary any happier to receive it.

The terse response opened Hillary's eyes to what the world was like outside her picture-perfect community of Park Ridge. Church leaders helped her further broaden her understanding. One youth minister, Donald Jones, played a particularly large role in that respect. Hillary said Jones "took us to meet black and Hispanic teenagers in downtown Chicago for service and worship exchanges. . . . Because my village was so secure, I had a hard time imagining what life was like for those in less fortunate circumstances."[18] In January 1963, Jones took Hillary and a few other students to Chicago's Orchestra Hall to hear a speech by Dr. Martin Luther King, Jr. Dr. King was a popular civil rights activist. He believed all people should be treated equally, regardless of the color of their skin. King's speech had a powerful effect on the fifteen year old. Hillary later said, "My youth minister from our church took a few of us down on a cold January night to hear someone that we had read about, we had watched on television, we had seen with our own eyes from a distance, this phenomenon known as Dr. King."[19] Seven months later, Dr. King led a march on Washington, D.C. There he delivered one of the most memorable speeches in history, which became known as his "I Have a Dream" speech.

As it did many people, Dr. King's work inspired Hillary. She continued her political involvement during her high school years. She attended Maine East High School as a freshman, sophomore, and junior. She was a

Martin Luther King, Jr., delivers his "I Have a Dream" speech on the steps of the Lincoln Memorial before more than 250,000 people in August 1963.

member of her student council and vice president of the junior class. As a senior, she attended Maine South High School. There she ran for student body president against several boys. One opponent told her she was crazy if she thought a girl could be elected president. Hillary lost the election but learned another valuable lesson about what roles the real world felt women should have.

Hillary soon joined a school group called Young Republicans. In 1964, she campaigned for Republican presidential candidate Barry Goldwater. She and the candidate's other young women supporters were called "Goldwater Girls." Goldwater lost the election to Democrat Lyndon B. Johnson. Johnson had once been John F. Kennedy's vice president and had become president when Kennedy was assassinated in 1963. Hillary's candidate may not have won, yet she had learned a lot about the way politics work. Years later, after Goldwater

A 1964 yearbook photo of Hillary Rodham (standing) and three classmates at Maine East High School.

learned Hillary had campaigned for him, he invited her to his home for a visit.[20]

Given her good grades and the expectations of her parents, it was clear Hillary was headed for college. The question was: Which one? Hillary had to decide. Two of her younger high school teachers helped guide her decision. Hillary said, "One had graduated from Wellesley and the other graduated from Smith. They'd been assigned to teach in my high school, and they were so bright and smart and terrific."[21] Hillary was inspired to be like them. She applied to both of the all-female schools, which encouraged women to become involved in politics and world affairs. The active student, ranked near the top of her class, was accepted to both. Her decision on which to attend came down to something simple. Hillary said, "I decided on Wellesley based on the photographs of the campus."[22] A picture, she thought, was worth a thousand words. That was one word for each mile she would have to travel to get to her new school.

3

SPEAKING OUT

Hillary and her parents made the long drive from Park Ridge, Illinois, to Wellesley, Massachusetts, for the first time in the fall of 1965. None of the Rodhams had been to the town of Wellesley. Still, the only Rodham daughter would be spending her next four years there. The family quickly discovered the town had a lot in common with Park Ridge. Like Park Ridge, Wellesley was an affluent suburb of a much-larger city, in this case Boston. Park Ridge and Wellesley also were similar in population, size, and wealth.

However, there were some differences between the two places. Unlike Park Ridge, Wellesley was home to two colleges. The one Hillary would be attending shared the name with the town. Located next to Lake Waban, Wellesley College was founded in 1870 with a goal of providing women a liberal, or wide-ranging, education. Those admitted to the school typically were the top students at their high schools, like Hillary. But that did not mean she fit in right away. Like many freshman, she knew no one at the school. The people she did meet seemed far different than those she had known in Park Ridge. Hillary said, "[Wellesley was] all very rich and fancy and very intimidating to my way of thinking."[1]

One reason Hillary felt that way is because many of the wealthiest families in the United States sent their children to Wellesley. The Rodhams were not poor, but neither were they extraordinarily rich. The trips she had taken to the poor parts of Chicago with her youth minister had introduced her to a lifestyle different from her own. Wellesley introduced her to the lifestyle of the very wealthy.

Day-to-day life at the college also was a lot different from what it had been in the schools Hillary grew up in. The environment at Wellesley was closely controlled. Students had many rules to follow. Their dorms were subject to nightly curfews. Men were allowed in those rooms for only a few hours on Sunday afternoons. When men visited, the dorm room door had to be kept open. Students also had to follow dress codes. At dinner, for example, girls had to wear skirts. The school's history played a role in its formality. Traditionally, Wellesley was known as a place where young women went to bide time until they married. Sure, they got a good education when

Hillary Rodham with one of her classmates at Wellesley College.

they were there. But, for many parents, making sure their daughters married well was their number one goal. One legend says members of Wellesley's senior class would compete to see who would be the first one to get married after graduation.[2]

Wellesley's classes proved to be difficult for Hillary, as well. Everything added up to make her feel like she did not belong. She said, "A month after school started, I called home collect and told my parents I didn't think I was smart enough to be there."[3] Her parents made her stay, and she quickly adjusted. Not having boys on campus helped. When she went to class, she did not worry about her looks, which allowed her to focus on learning. NASA told her she could not become an astronaut. In high school, she was told there was no way a girl could win the position of student body president. But at Wellesley, she could be anything she wanted to be. In time, she did just that.

Hillary soon was elected president of Wellesley's Young Republicans. The selection made a lot of sense, since she had been a member of a similar group in high school. She also had grown up supporting and working for Republicans. But, despite her experience with the party, Hillary soon began wondering if being a Republican was the right choice. She said, "My doubts about the party and its policies were growing, particularly when it came to civil rights and the Vietnam War."[4]

The Vietnam War

The Vietnam War began in 1957 as a battle between North Vietnam and South Vietnam. The North was under control of the Communist Party and hoped to take over the non-Communist South. North Vietnam's goal was to overthrow South Vietnam's government and rejoin the two into one Vietnam. The United States was strongly against Communism and did not want this to happen. So, the United States joined the war in the 1960s and sent hundreds of thousands of soldiers to help the South. As the war dragged on, more and more American soldiers were killed.

Back home, Americans were divided on the war. Some believed the United States should be involved. Others believed it should not be. In time, the number of Americans killed in Vietnam grew and support for the war declined. Families were losing their friends and loved ones. Soon, Americans began rallying for the war to end. In 1973, the United States government brought its soldiers home. Estimates say fifty-eight thousand American soldiers were killed in Vietnam, and three hundred thousand were wounded.[5] Two million Vietnamese civilians and soldiers were killed.[6]

Hillary said, "It's hard to explain to young Americans today . . . how obsessed many in my generation were with the Vietnam War. . . . The country was divided, leaving us confused about our own feelings. My friends and I constantly discussed and debated it."[7] Although the war ended in 1975, it still evokes strong feelings in people. Many soldiers have never been accounted for.

Troops patrol during a seek-and-destroy mission to locate Viet Cong near Ben-Cat, Vietnam, in 1970. The U.S. finally withdrew from Vietnam in 1973. The war ended in 1975.

Soon, Hillary resigned as president of the Young Republicans. She was not only beginning to disagree with the Republican Party, but she was also at odds with President Johnson, a Democrat. Johnson supported the Vietnam War even after many Americans, including Hillary, began to think the country should no longer be involved.

During her junior year at Wellesley, Hillary Rodham began campaigning for Democrat Eugene McCarthy. McCarthy was seeking the 1968 Democratic presidential nomination. He also was strongly against the Vietnam War. On weekends, Rodham drove to New Hampshire to help McCarthy's campaign. Many college students who were frustrated with the war did the same. New Hampshire's primary elections were to be the first held in the United States. Doing well in that state would get any presidential candidate off to a good start. Even with the students's help, McCarthy eventually lost the party's nomination to Vice President Hubert Humphrey. But he did fare well in New Hampshire, where Rodham and others had helped. The experience kept Rodham's interest in politics high.

The summer before her senior year of college, Rodham was chosen to be an intern in Washington, D.C. Working in the country's capital city was a great opportunity for Rodham. She was seeking a degree in political science—the study of politics— and Washington, D.C., is the center of the country's political machine. Rodham certainly was grateful for the opportunity, but only to a point. She objected when she was assigned to work with Republican members of Congress. But if she wanted to remain in the program she had to work with her former party. She decided to do so and went to work for Republican congressman Harold Collier from her home state of Illinois. When the internship was over, the person in charge of the program had good things to say about Rodham. He said, "She presented her viewpoints very forcibly, always had ideas, always defended what she had in mind."[8]

While in Washington, D.C., Rodham and a few others were asked to go to Miami to the Republican National Convention. They were there to help New York Governor Nelson Rockefeller win his party's presidential nomination. Rockefeller was not a Democrat, but Rodham went anyway. The candidate eventually lost the Republican nomination to Richard Nixon. Nixon went on to become the thirty-seventh president of the United States.

When Rodham's work was done, she returned to her family's home in Park Ridge for the rest of the summer. During that time, she traveled with friend Betsy Johnson into Chicago during the Democratic National Convention. For several reasons, the country was suffering great unrest. Dr. Martin Luther King, Jr., whose speech had inspired Rodham five years earlier, recently had been assassinated. She took the news of his death hard. Her college roommate said Rodham entered the room crying and threw her book bag into a wall. Then she shouted, "I can't stand it anymore! I can't take anymore!"[9]

An important senator who was running for president, Robert Kennedy, the former attorney general of the United States and brother of assassinated president John F. Kennedy, had also been recently killed. The Vietnam War still was being fought, and many soldiers were dying.

For those reasons and others, many people were upset with the government. So they decided to protest during the convention. Those protestors, and police, were fighting everywhere. Riots broke out and several people were arrested. Rodham said, "Betsy and I were shocked by the police brutality we saw."[10] Her friend was even more explicit. She said, "We saw kids our age getting their heads beaten in. And the police were doing the beating. Hillary and I just looked at each other. We had had a wonderful childhood in Park Ridge, but we obviously hadn't gotten the whole story."[11]

By the time she entered her senior year at Wellesley, Rodham was a full-fledged Democrat. She also had decided to go to law school to become a lawyer. Now, she had to pick a school. Just as she had when choosing a college four years prior, Rodham narrowed her choices to two. This time it was Yale and Harvard. Both colleges were part of the Ivy League, considered to be one of the top groups of schools in the country. Rodham was having a hard time making her final decision. Because it was only a few miles away from Wellesley, Harvard made a lot of sense. That is until Rodham went to a reception at the school. After she was introduced to one of Harvard's professors, her mind was made up. The professor said, "First of all, we have no nearest competitor, and, secondly, we don't need any more women."[12] Not surprisingly, Rodham chose Yale.

First, she had to complete her senior year at Wellesley. She was elected president of the Class of 1969. She was very active in this role and even invited Saul Alinsky to speak to the student body. Alinsky was controversial but well known for being a motivational speaker capable of organizing people together to rally for change. Rodham also interviewed Alinsky for her senior thesis, or research project.

As the end of the school year neared, one of Rodham's classmates suggested it would be nice to have a student speak during their graduation ceremony. The problem was it had never been done before. Rodham's friend told the school's president, Ruth Adams, that her class would like to have a speaker. The president initially said no, but finally decided to hear more when she was told the students might hold their own ceremony if they did not get their way. As class president, Rodham took it from there. She asked Adams why she was against letting a student speak. She also told her she was the one chosen to speak. A few days before graduation, Adams finally agreed with the students. After nearly one hundred years,

Wellesley would have a student speak at graduation. The pressure was on Rodham, who had no idea what she was going to say. She had little time to figure it out. Her classmates proved to be a big help. As she was writing her speech, her friends were sliding notes with their ideas under the door of her dorm room.[13]

Preparing to become the first-ever student graduation speaker was not the only stress Rodham was going through. Her mother was sick back home in Park Ridge and could not travel to see her daughter graduate. Her busy father was not going to attend, either, but when he heard his daughter was going to speak, Hugh Rodham decided to go. Adding to Rodham's stress was the knowledge of who would be speaking before her—United States Senator Edward Brooke. Three years earlier, when Rodham was still a Republican, she had campaigned to get Brooke elected. Now, she was going to be speaking on the same stage. The two disagreed on many issues.

During the ceremony, Rodham listened intently to the senator's speech. When he finished, she felt let down. He had not talked about any of the issues she felt her generation was struggling with, such as the Vietnam War and civil rights. "The Senator seemed out of touch with his audience," Rodham later wrote in her autobiography. "His words were aimed at a different Wellesley, one that predated the upheavals of the 1960s."[14]

Dressed in cap and gown and wearing her familiar oversized glasses, Rodham began her speech. First, she talked about issues she believed the senator should have addressed. Her words encouraged students to continue to protest, even though the senator said not to. Her speech argued against many of the ideas Senator Brooke had spoken about minutes earlier. Rodham's speech elicited reactions from nearly all of the two thousand people in the audience. In general, the older people felt uncomfortable and the younger people were inspired. But nobody was unmoved when she said she would like to see a world where people were treated as more than just numbers.

When Rodham finished, the front rows of the crowd stood and applauded. Those were her classmates. They cheered their rebellious class president for seven straight minutes.[15] Others were silent, shocked that a

Hillary Rodham at her commencement ceremony at Wellesley. Senator Brooke stands at the far right.

twenty-one-year-old woman had spoken such harsh words in front of, and about, a well-known politician. Rodham herself was shocked over the next few days, as the media started to report on how she had upstaged a popular senator.

But what she said had been important—to her classmates, the audience and, soon, to the entire United States. The impact of her words even surprised Rodham. She said, "I had no idea my speech would generate interest far beyond Wellesley. . . . When I called home, however, my mother told me that she had been fielding phone calls from reporters and television shows asking me for interviews and appearances."[16] Rodham ended up granting some of those requests. *Life* magazine featured her as one of the voices of her generation. She also appeared on a TV show in Chicago. The speech made the young woman a celebrity. Few knew the speech was not supposed to happen just a few days earlier.

Rodham did not bask in the spotlight for long. After graduation, in fact, she moved far from it. She spent the summer working in Alaska. There, she washed dishes and worked in a fish plant. She was fired from the fish plant when she pointed out that some of the fish looked rotten. Rodham said, "When I told the manager, he fired me and told me to come back the next afternoon to pick up my last check."[17] Rodham said when she showed up the next day, the entire business was gone.

4
TWO LAW
STUDENTS

Rodham moved to New Haven, Connecticut, in the fall of 1969 to begin her first year at Yale Law School. Her new school was similar to the one she had just graduated from in many ways. Both colleges had long histories of being among the best in the country. Both also were known to be quite wealthy. At the 126-year-old law school, just as there had been at Wellesley and other colleges across the country, there was a lot of political unrest. Organized student protests were not uncommon.

However, female students were still fairly uncommon. Rodham was one of twenty-seven women accepted to the law school. Two hundred and eight men were. That year, 1969, Yale admitted its first group of female undergraduates. Women in America were becoming empowered. It was just happening slowly.

She may have come from an all-women's college, but Rodham was up for the challenge of competing with the men of Yale. The celebrity status she had achieved from her graduation speech helped boost her confidence.

Rodham continued tackling issues such as civil rights and the Vietnam War during her first year at Yale Law School. Nationally, a couple of key events related to those issues occurred during the year. In April 1970, eight Black Panthers (an African-American civil rights group) were put on trial in New Haven. The Black Panthers were accused of murder, but many felt the government had set them up. When the trials took place, thousands of angry people gathered in the city to protest.

Rodham also was deeply affected by what happened in Kent, Ohio, that May. Hundreds of demonstrators gathered at Kent State University to protest President Nixon's announcement that the United States was expanding the Vietnam War into the country of Cambodia. The Kent State protests quickly grew out of hand. Some demonstrators set fires, threw bottles, and cursed at police. The governor called in the National Guard to regain order, but it did not help much. On May 4, members of the National Guard shot and killed four students and injured several others.

Rodham cried over the situation. She said, "I remember rushing out the door of the law school in tears."[1] Rodham had always advocated the right to protest, but she also believed those protests should be peaceful. She never wanted them to end as they had at Kent State University.

Rodham did not have long to focus on the negative. Three days after the shootings, she spoke at a League of Women Voters meeting in Washington, D.C. She made an important connection there. The main speaker was a woman named Marian Wright Edelman. Edelman was a graduate of Yale Law School and an activist. She had started a group that would later become the Children's Defense Fund. She offered Rodham a summer job but did not have money to pay her. Rodham felt strongly about what Edelman was trying to accomplish, so she got a grant to

Marian Edelman speaks during a news conference on February 14, 1983.

pay for her to live in Washington, D.C, and took the job. Edelman's work had a huge impact on the college student. Rodham said, "I knew right away that I had to go to work for her."[2] In part, the job involved researching the lives of poor children. The experience of working with children had an impact on Rodham. So much so, in fact, that when she returned to Yale, she decided to focus her studies on children's rights.

Shortly into her second year in law school, another matter captured Rodham's attention. This time, it was a handsome law student from Arkansas. His name was Bill Clinton. There was an obvious attraction between the two from the beginning. Both later said they had seen each other around campus a few times and each had found the other attractive. But for a long time they did not talk to each other. That is, until one day in the library.

After catching Clinton staring at her, Rodham decided to break the ice. She said, "If you're going to keep staring at me and I'm going to keep staring back, we ought to at least know each other's names. Mine's Hillary Rodham. What's yours?"[3] The two talked for a short time, and then Rodham left. A few days later, they ran into each other again. Rodham was on her way to register for classes. Clinton said that was where he was going, too. In reality, he had already registered. He just wanted to spend time with Rodham. When the two got to the front of the line, the worker said, "Bill, what are you doing back here? You registered this morning."[4] Clinton was caught. Rodham laughed at her crush's lie. Soon, they were dating.

Rodham and Clinton were from different backgrounds. Rodham had grown up in what was considered a traditional American family, with mother and father married, living in a house in the suburbs. Clinton was born in the poor city of Hope, Arkansas, as William Jefferson Blythe III. Clinton's father died in an accident three months before his son was born on August 19, 1946. Four years later, the young boy's mother married a car salesman named Roger Clinton. Roger Clinton officially adopted Bill when he was in his teens. It was a warming gesture, but

Hillary Rodham and Bill Clinton on the campus of Yale in the early 1970s.

the family's lives still were nowhere near perfect. Bill Clinton described his stepfather as abusive and violent, especially when he drank alcohol. Bill's mother often would remove him and his younger brother from the house to protect them. In a book he wrote years later, Bill Clinton described one terrifying fight between his mother and stepfather. He said, "They were screaming at each other in their bedroom . . . I walked out into the hall to the doorway of the bedroom. Just as I did [the stepfather] pulled a gun from behind his back and fired in Mother's direction."[5] The bullet landed in the wall between mother and child. The police were called and Roger Clinton was taken to jail. The couple eventually divorced. Later, Bill Clinton's mother remarried.

Through his tumultuous childhood, Bill Clinton somehow remained a good student. By the time he met Rodham, he had graduated from Georgetown University in Washington, D.C. He also had won a prestigious Rhodes Scholarship, which took him to England to study. Though they came from different backgrounds, both Clinton and Rodham were well educated.

Both students also had a strong interest in politics. Clinton had known since he was a teenager that he wanted to serve the public. Rodham also had been involved with politics since she was young. The couple soon became inseparable and moved into an apartment together before Rodham's third year at Yale. In the summer of 1972, they moved together to Texas to work to get

George McGovern, a Democratic senator from South Dakota, elected president. McGovern lost the race, but both Rodham and Clinton made some important political connections during his campaign.

Students typically graduate from law school in three years. Rodham decided to postpone her law degree for a year to study child development. So, her final year at Yale was mainly spent working on issues close to her heart. She did research at the Yale Child Study Center and worked with foster families at the New Haven Legal Services office. She even helped write a book. The extra year in school also allowed her to spend more time with Clinton.

Rodham and Clinton graduated from Yale Law School in the spring of 1973. They then flew to England to visit many of the places Clinton had seen during his time studying there. At the end of the trip, they stopped at Lake District National Park. There, on the shores of a glacier-fed lake named Ennerdale, Clinton asked Rodham to marry him.

Rodham had known the question would someday come. She also had known there would not be an easy answer because both had ambitious career goals. She planned to be a big-city lawyer in someplace like New York City or Washington, D.C. Clinton planned to go back to his home state of Arkansas to become a politician. Clinton's question forced Rodham to make an important life decision. Would she choose her career or love? Rodham said, "I was desperately in love with him but utterly confused about my life and future. So I said, 'No, not now.' What I meant was, 'Give me time.' "6

When the couple returned to the United States, they took a brief trip to Arkansas so Rodham could visit the state where Clinton had grown up and where he would soon be living again. He had accepted a job to teach at the University of Arkansas Law School in Fayetteville. There, he would plan the political career he had talked about since he was a teen. When summer ended, the pair moved apart.

Rodham moved back to Massachusetts to begin her plan of working with children. Marian Wright Edelman, whom Rodham had worked for in the summer of 1970, hired her as an attorney for the Children's Defense Fund. The job required a lot of traveling. On the road, Rodham sometimes visited children in deplorable conditions. She said, "I found children who weren't in school because of physical disabilities like blindness and deafness. . . . I met a girl in a wheelchair, who told me how much she wanted to go to school. She knew she couldn't go because she couldn't walk."7 The experience broke her heart, but Rodham still loved her job because she believed she was making a difference.

Rodham's other passion was fifteen hundred miles away. Bill Clinton had decided to give politics a try sooner than most expected. He announced a run for the U.S. House of Representatives. It was obvious he was planning to stay in Arkansas. If Rodham wanted to be with him, she would have to move. She strongly considered it. She had passed the Arkansas bar exam, so she would be allowed to practice law in that state. It appeared love was going to win out over her big-city aspirations. But a phone call in January 1974 stopped her from moving.

The House Judiciary Committee, a branch of the House of Representatives, recently had selected attorney John Doar to lead the impeachment proceedings against President Nixon. If Nixon were impeached, he would be removed from office. The Republican president had been accused of hiring burglars to spy on Democrats, then trying to cover it up. The scandal was called Watergate, after the Washington, D.C., building where the crimes had taken place. Watergate was most famously known as a hotel but also housed many offices, including the offices of the Democratic National Committee that were broken into.

Doar needed a team of lawyers to assist him with the impeachment process. He called Bill Clinton to ask if he wanted to help. Clinton was not interested in moving to Washington, D.C., for the job. Doar called the next person on his list: Hillary Rodham. The opportunity to work on a case against a United States president was too good for Rodham to refuse. She took the job and moved to Washington, D.C. There, she worked with a team of forty-four lawyers. The hours were long and the team worked seven days a week to build a case against President Nixon. When a tape recording of the president rehearsing lies about the break-in was released in August 1974, Rodham's job was all but over. That evidence was so strong, the president knew he would most likely be convicted of the crimes he was charged with. So, on August 9, 1974, Nixon resigned from office.

Nixon's resignation officially ended Rodham's job. She had no idea what she was going to do next. She decided to act on an earlier offer to teach law at the University of Arkansas. Finally, she and Clinton could be together again. Rodham said, "I knew I was happier with Bill than without him."[8]

The resignation of President Nixon (below) in the wake of the Watergate scandal in 1974 was a seminal event in U.S. politics.

Many people did not want Rodham to move to Fayetteville. Because Arkansas was generally considered a poor state located in the middle of "nowhere," Rodham's friends thought she was crazy to go there. She could work anywhere in the country, so why there? Clinton's family, especially his mother, Virginia, also did not want Rodham to move to Fayetteville. His mother thought Rodham was too plain and did not care enough about appearances. Clinton's mother spent a lot of time on her own looks and expected other women to do the same. For that reason and others, she felt Rodham was not good enough for her son. Some of Clinton's congressional campaign staff members also did not like the idea of having Rodham around. They thought she would be a distraction and hurt his chances of getting elected.

Stubborn and in love, Rodham went anyway. She moved into her own house and began teaching at the university. She also helped Clinton's campaign. In November, Clinton lost a close election. Afterward, he resumed his teaching job.

In the summer of 1975, Clinton drove Rodham to the airport so she could visit friends in Chicago and on the East Coast. On the way, the couple passed a small brick house with a "For Sale" sign in the front yard. As they drove past, Rodham mentioned how much she liked the place, which was priced at $20,500. When she returned from her trip, Clinton picked her up at the airport. He asked if she remembered the house. Then he said, "I bought it. You have to marry me now, because I can't live there alone."[9] After two years of being asked and answering that she was not ready, Rodham finally said yes.

Their engagement was short. The couple married in the small house's living room on October 11, 1975. Two months later, they honeymooned in Acapulco, Mexico, with Rodham's two brothers and parents along. Though most women took the last name of their husband after marriage, Rodham decided to keep hers. "I need to maintain my interests and my commitments. I need my own identity, too," she said.[10]

Back home in Arkansas, the newlyweds resumed their teaching jobs. But Clinton was nowhere near ready to give up politics. In May 1976, he decided to run for attorney general of Arkansas. The attorney general is the head law officer and legal adviser to the government. In November, Clinton was elected to the position. He and Rodham sold their little house and moved to the state capital of Little Rock.

Moving meant Rodham had to give up her job at the university. She decided to go into private practice and was hired by the Rose Law Firm. One of the firm's partners was a man named Vince Foster. Rodham had met Foster while teaching at the University of Arkansas. She continued working for children's rights with the firm and went to trial in several cases. As had happened many other times, the pressure was on Rodham at her new job.

Hillary and Bill Clinton on their wedding day on October 11, 1975.

She was the first female lawyer the highly respected law firm had ever hired. She was also the main breadwinner for her family. Clinton may have been in a powerful government position, but the job did not pay well. Rodham had to pay for many of their expenses.

Being the wife of a well-known public official brought Rodham a lot of attention. She said, "Wives of elected officials were constantly scrutinized."[11] The unwanted attention reaffirmed what her mother-in-law had told her: Appearances were important to people in the South. That was good for Clinton. His charm, wit, and boyish good looks had made him a popular attorney general and helped him get elected. He was so popular, in fact, that he decided to run for governor. After winning the Democratic nomination, he went on to be elected to the position. At age thirty-two, he was the youngest governor in the United States.

The following year, Rodham became a partner, or equal, at her law firm in Arkansas. The president of the United States, Jimmy Carter, had even appointed her to the board of a corporation that gave legal assistance to the poor. Rodham and her new husband had achieved a lot in the five years since they had graduated from law school. As young as they were, more success was certain to come. What they did not know was that there would be many tough times as well.

5
FIRST LADY OF ARKANSAS

Bill Clinton took office as governor of Arkansas in January 1979. A short time later, he and Rodham achieved another of their major goals when Rodham became pregnant. Chelsea Victoria Clinton was born February 27, 1980. The baby's name came from the song "Chelsea Morning," by singer-songwriter Joni Mitchell. They chose the name years earlier, when they were listening to the song while walking through the beautiful Chelsea neighborhood of London.

Rodham had no intention of quitting her job as a lawyer to be a full-time first lady and mother. Yet she did take four months off work to stay home with her new daughter. Her bonding experience with Chelsea led her to believe even more strongly that working women should be allowed to have some paid time off after giving birth. She was fortunate enough to be able to do that. She knew many women could not.

Keeping her job turned out to be a wise move. In 1980, Clinton lost his re-election bid. So, in the beginning of 1981, the family moved out of the Governor's Mansion. They bought a house in Little Rock, and Clinton took a job with a local law firm.

Over the years, the pressure on Rodham from family and the general public to change her last name continued to grow. When Rodham's mother sent letters to the couple, she addressed them to "Mr. and Mrs. Bill Clinton."[1] Clinton's mother felt so strongly about the issue that she had cried when she was told Rodham was not changing her name.[2] Equally important was the reaction from the general public. A lot of people felt it was odd for a woman to keep her maiden name after marriage. It was not at all common at the time. When Clinton decided to again run for governor in 1982, Rodham made her own big decision. Despite believing a name should not matter, she decided to change hers. Hillary Rodham became Hillary Clinton. She said, "It was not a decision that was easy to make for me, but it was one that I made, thinking it was the best for me and the best for my husband."[3] She wanted the criticism to end.

Hillary Clinton also changed her appearance. She replaced her big-framed glasses with contact lenses. She began wearing more fashionable clothes. She even

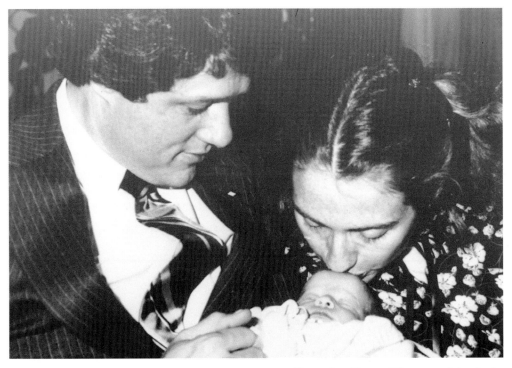

Bill and Hillary Clinton with their newborn daughter, Chelsea.

updated her hairstyle. How much it all helped is unknown, but, with a lot of campaign assistance from his wife, Bill Clinton won the election. He was again governor. The family moved out of their private home and back into the Governor's Mansion. The help Hillary gave her husband to become governor also helped her. Bill selected Hillary to head the Arkansas Education Standards Committee. The group's main focus was on the quality of education across the state. Big changes were needed in that area, because Arkansas residents were among the poorest and least educated in America. Given Hillary's experience with educational issues, the job was perfect. With her help, important legislation to reform Arkansas schools passed the Legislature. For that and other reasons, a newspaper chose Hillary Clinton as its Arkansas Woman of the Year in 1984.

Bill Clinton kept getting re-elected and remained governor of Arkansas until 1992, a total of twelve years. His popularity was extremely high during that time. He was so well liked, in fact, that many encouraged him to run for president in 1988. He considered it but decided not to. Republican George H. W. Bush won that year's election to become the forty-first president of the United States.

The Clintons remained in Arkansas and continued to help that state grow. Hillary Clinton achieved many great things as first lady. She brought a program called HIPPY to the state. It stood for Home Instruction Program for Preschool Youngsters. The program helped get young preschool-aged children ready to enter the school system. Hillary Clinton also remained involved with the Children's Defense Fund.

In many ways, life as a Clinton appeared to be perfect. Those appearances were deceiving. During his years in office, Bill Clinton had gained a reputation as a womanizer, a man who has an interest in many women. Rumors were everywhere. The most notorious relationship he had was with a woman named Gennifer Flowers. Flowers met Clinton in 1977, when she was working as a television reporter. She later claimed she had an affair with Clinton for more than ten years. Clinton denied it for a long time. Years later, he admitted he had an affair with Flowers. Some say Hillary knew her husband was seeing other women and chose to ignore it. Others think she did not know. Hillary has addressed the issue several times. She once said, "I don't talk about it. I think my marriage is my marriage and my relationship with my husband is solely between us."[4]

If people knew about Bill Clinton's alleged woman-izing, they did not seem to care much. He remained a popular governor. Meanwhile, President Bush grew unpopular with many citizens. Pressure on Clinton to run for the country's highest office again grew. Chelsea's

Former Arkansas first ladies at the grand opening of The William J. Clinton Center in Little Rock in November 2004. From left to right: Gay White, Hillary Clinton, Barbara Pryor, Betty Bumpers, Janet Huckabee, and Betty Tucker.

age was one of the reasons he had decided not to run in 1988. His daughter was only seven at that time and being president is a time-consuming duty. Clinton said he did not want to be away from his daughter as much as he would be if he were president. But Chelsea was eleven when the next election cycle came around, and the Clintons had spent a lot of time getting her ready for the amount of negative attention their family would receive during a presidential race. To prepare, one parent would pretend to say bad things about the other to teach Chelsea how to react. Hillary Clinton told her daughter, "By the time this is over, they'll attack you, they'll attack your cat, they'll attack your goldfish."[5]

Chelsea said she could handle the pressure and encouraged her father to run for president. In September 1991, Bill Clinton made up his mind: he would enter the presidential race. The announcement speech he made on October 3 in Little Rock made it official. He said, "Today I am declaring my candidacy for President of the United States. Together I believe we can provide leadership that will restore the American dream—that will fight for the forgotten middle class—that will provide more opportunity, insist on more responsibility and create a greater sense of community for this great country."[6] His inspirational message of hope was similar to what Hillary had said years ago in her college graduation speech. Clinton hoped it would be as successful as his wife's had been.

Bill and Hillary Clinton with their daughter, Chelsea, in Little Rock, Arkansas, on October 3, 1991, shortly after Governor Clinton announced his bid for the presidency.

Some in Arkansas were upset by Clinton's announcement. They had voted him governor because he promised he would complete his term in that office. If elected president, he could not do that. But Clinton felt he could spread his mission to a wider audience as president. Besides, running for president is not an opportunity many get. Others in Arkansas were supportive and happy to see someone from their state run for president. Clinton also had a powerful and successful team member built in. Hillary Clinton said, "If you vote for my husband, you get me; it's a two-for-one, blue-plate special."[7] Many believed Hillary Clinton was helping her husband so much behind the scenes they were basically one person. Soon, the nickname of "Billary" was used to describe the two.

6
PRESIDENTIAL CAMPAIGN

Bill Clinton was wildly popular in Arkansas. He had made a lot of positive changes there during his days as governor. But the forty-five-year-old still was not expected to win the Democratic nomination for president. Hardly anyone outside Arkansas knew who he was. His biggest exposure to a national audience had come a few years earlier, when he had been asked to give the nominating speech for presidential candidate Michael Dukakis. Clinton's speech was too long. People began yelling at him to hurry up and finish. Hillary Clinton said, "Many observers assumed Bill's political future was over."[1] It was not. Now, he was a candidate for the country's highest office.

The allegations of Bill Clinton's womanizing followed him into his candidacy. Gennifer Flowers had tape-recorded some conversations she had with him. The recordings made Clinton appear guilty of having an affair with her. A tabloid magazine soon wrote that she and Clinton had been seeing each other for more than a decade. Other media outlets began reporting similar stories. Flowers became a celebrity. Television stations, newspapers, and magazines all wanted her to talk to them. Eventually, she wrote a book telling her story.

When the Flowers tapes were released, many thought Clinton's chances of becoming president were over. But Hillary Clinton felt her husband had done nothing wrong. She believed someone, most likely the Republican Party, was trying to ruin Bill's chances of becoming president by paying Flowers to say what she said. Hillary said of Flowers's story, "It's not true. I just don't believe any of that. All of these people, including that woman, have denied this many, many times. I'm not going to speculate on her motive. We know she was paid."[2]

People wanted answers. If he was innocent, why would he, a married man, spend so much time talking to another woman on the telephone? Hillary Clinton had an explanation. She said, "Anybody who knows my husband knows that he bends over backwards to help people who are in trouble and is always willing to listen to their problems."[3]

If they wanted to save Bill's chances of becoming president, the Clintons had to act out against the negative publicity. In January 1992, they went on a national television program to talk about the Flowers situation. Their interview was shown immediately after the Super Bowl, one of the most-watched programs of the year. The interviewer asked Bill Clinton if he had an affair with Flowers. Clinton said, "The allegation is false."[4] Years later, in a sworn statement, Clinton admitted he had an affair with Flowers. But at the time of the interview, he was still claiming his innocence, and his wife was backing him up. When the interviewer referred to the couple's marriage as an "arrangement," Hillary Clinton became visibly upset. She said, " I'm not sitting here—some little woman standing by her man like Tammy Wynette. I'm sitting here because I love him, and I honor what we've been through together. . . . If that's not enough for people, then heck, don't vote for him."[5]

Hillary Clinton's reference to Tammy Wynette upset the famous country singer and many of her fans. Wynette demanded an apology. By "standing by her man," Hillary was referring to a song Wynette had written in the 1960s called "Stand by Your Man." The woman in the song stood by her man when he did something she did not "understand," but Wynette herself was a strong woman. She found Hillary Clinton's comment insulting. Clinton later apologized. She said, "I didn't mean to hurt Tammy Wynette as a person. I happen to be a country-western fan. If she feels like I've hurt her feelings, I'm sorry about that."[6] The controversy was another hard lesson for the Clintons. They had been in the public eye a lot of their lives. They had dealt with the media asking them personal questions. But the scrutiny the Clintons received when Bill became a presidential candidate was greater than they ever had experienced. Even when Hillary did something as simple as change her hairstyle, it became a story somewhere.

For the Clintons, the Tammy Wynette and Gennifer Flowers incidents were the beginning of a lot more negative publicity. In February 1992, the *Wall Street Journal* newspaper ran an article that angered many people. It claimed Bill Clinton had dodged the draft during the Vietnam War. Today, serving in the military is strictly voluntary. People choose to join or not. But, during the Vietnam War, all young men were required to join the armed forces if the government drafted them to. For a variety of reasons, many young men did not want to join the military. Some did not want to have to risk their lives in conflict during wartime. Others disagreed with the war or generally were against violence of any kind.

To avoid serving, young men used several means to "dodge" the draft. Some sought deferments, or legal exemptions, to avoid being drafted. Those included medical and educational reasons. Others tried to join the National Guard or military reserve units, which seldom went to war. Some draft dodgers left the country. Many Americans have strong beliefs that those called upon

Bill and Hillary Clinton appear at the St. Patrick's Day Parade in Chicago on March 15, 1992.

should serve their country if they are selected. These people were upset with the allegation that Bill Clinton had dodged the draft. Clinton's reputation suffered because of it.

Through it all, there was a presidential race going on. Amazingly, Bill Clinton remained in the battle. But he still was only one of several Democrats trying to win the party's nomination. The candidates traveled the country trying to win voters. They attacked each other personally. They attacked each other professionally. The negative aspects of the campaign were exactly what the Clintons had warned their daughter about. But Bill Clinton fought through them. And by June it became clear: he would win the Democratic Party's nomination for the 1992 presidential election.

There was little time to rest or celebrate. Of the three main presidential candidates, Bill Clinton was third in the polls. The current president, Republican George H. W. Bush, was running again and was more popular than Clinton. Another man, Ross Perot, was more popular, too. There was a lot of work to be done.

First, Clinton chose a United States senator from Tennessee, Al Gore, as his running mate. Gore would become vice president if Clinton were elected president. Gore was similar to Bill Clinton in many ways. Hillary Clinton and Gore's wife, Tipper, also had a lot in common. Both were accomplished, independent, opinionated, and powerful women. Tipper Gore had achieved some level of celebrity in the 1980s, when she co-founded the Parents Music Resource Center (PMRC). The group believed the lyrics of popular rock 'n' roll songs were too full of sex and violence. They said such songs were a bad influence on society and responsible for many of its ills. Popular rock musicians fought against the PMRC, but the group successfully campaigned against record labels to have them put warning stickers on music albums.

President-elect Bill Clinton, his wife Hillary and daughter Chelsea step out onto the podium at the Old State House in Little Rock, Arkansas, in the early morning hours of November 4, 1992, shortly after President Bush conceded the election to him.

In July, the Clintons and Gores began touring across the United States in a bus. Hillary named the tour "Bill, Al, Hillary and Tipper's Excellent Adventures,"[7] after a popular movie of the time. The candidates and their wives traveled the country and talked to voters along the way. The two couples hardly knew each other when they began but grew close to each other on the trip.

In addition to the bus campaign, the Clintons flew to several states to speak to voters. In November, the hard work paid off. Bill Clinton defeated both President Bush and Perot in the election. Clinton received forty-three percent of the popular, or citizen, votes. Less than half of Americans had chosen him on their ballots. Many critics held this fact against Clinton throughout the course of his presidency.

When President Bush called to concede the 1992 race, Hillary Clinton said, "I was overwhelmed . . . Bill and I went into our bedroom, closed the door and prayed together for God's help as he took on this awesome honor and responsibility."[8]

Bill Clinton was about to become the forty-second President of the United States. He was only forty-six years old. He had been a young governor. Now, he was going to be a young president. Hillary Clinton would be the country's first lady. Many wondered exactly what she would do in that position. She did, too. She said, "I had to decide what I wanted to do with the opportunities and responsibilities I had inherited."[9] As she usually did, Hillary Clinton made the most of those opportunities.

7

A BUSY FIRST LADY

With his twelve-year-old daughter and his wife at his side, Bill Clinton was sworn in as President of the United States in January 1993. The chilly winter weather in Washington, D.C., did not stop people from showing up to see their new leader. Thousands gathered at the Capitol to witness the historic event. During his speech, Clinton talked of changes he felt needed to be made to the country. He said, "A new season of American renewal has begun. To renew America, we must be bold. We must do what no generation has had to do before. We must invest more in our own people, in their jobs, in their future, and at the same time cut our massive debt. And we must do so in a world in which we must compete for every opportunity."[1]

The swearing-in ceremony was not the only celebration held for the new president. There also was an inaugural gala that featured many famous stars. Bob Dylan, Aretha Franklin, Kenny Rogers, Diana Ross, Barbara Streisand, Elizabeth Taylor, Stevie Wonder, and others were there. At the end of the gala, the Clintons and Gores sang the song "We Are the World" with pop music legend Michael Jackson. The next day there was a parade, followed by several inaugural balls held in the president's honor. Bill and Hillary made appearances at every one before returning to their new home long after midnight.

The family's belongings had been shipped from Arkansas to the White House immediately after Bill Clinton was sworn into office. Hillary Clinton was no stranger to the massive building she was about to call home. She had been inside before. But she still was overwhelmed by her new home and life. She said, "It was during my walk up the path toward the White House . . . that the reality hit me: I was actually the First Lady, married to the President of the United States."[2]

The White House even had a new pet, the Clintons's family cat, Socks. The cat was nearly as popular with the public as the Clintons. Hillary said, "The two most common questions I'm asked . . . are how is Chelsea and how is Socks. That is what I'm always asked, no matter what group I'm in."[3] A few years later, the Clintons

President Bill Clinton and Vice President Al Gore greets visitors in the Diplomatic Reception Room of the White House on Thursday, January 2, 1993, during an open house on the new administration's first full day in office.

added a chocolate Labrador retriever named Buddy to their White House family.

Once the celebrations died down, the Clintons went to work. When Bill was governor of Arkansas, he had appointed his wife to a job leading an important education committee. This time, laws would not allow him to appoint her to a high-level position. It is not as if she

The White House

The White House, located at 1600 Pennsylvania Avenue in Washington, D.C., is one of the best-known buildings in the United States. The country's first president, George Washington, ordered construction to begin in 1792. Sadly, the building was not completed during Washington's lifetime. The first presidential couple to live there was John Adams and his wife, Abigail. They began living there in 1800. The presidential mansion was not called the White House until one hundred one years later. The inside of the building is fifty-five thousand square feet, roughly the size of an entire city block. There are one hundred thirty-two rooms, thirty-five bathrooms, twenty-eight fireplaces, a running track, a movie theater, a bowling lane and a swimming pool. The White House kitchen has five full-time chefs.[4]

needed something to keep her busy. For Hillary Clinton, being the first lady was a full-time job. It was her decision for it to be that way.

Throughout history, first ladies have played a variety of roles. Some, such as Dwight D. Eisenhower's wife, Mamie, chose to maintain a low profile. A former Army wife, Mamie Eisenhower was used to moving around to wherever her husband's job took her. Her main role had always been to maintain the family home as a housewife. When her husband became the thirty-fourth president in 1953, she continued playing that role. She hosted lavish dinners at the White House but excused herself when her husband talked about official matters.[5] Barbara Bush, the woman who preceded Hillary Clinton as first lady, took a behind-the-scenes role similar to Mamie Eisenhower's.

In contrast, several first ladies were very much in the public eye. One of the most well known was Jacqueline

Kennedy, wife of the thirty-fifth United States president, John F. Kennedy. The glamorous woman was nearly always the center of attention. However, like Mamie Eisenhower, she preferred to not meddle in her husband's affairs. She said her husband "wouldn't—and couldn't have a wife who shared the spotlight with him."[6]

Hillary Clinton's time as first lady promised to be different than Mamie Eisenhower's, Barbara Bush's, and Jacqueline Kennedy's. She was not a traditional home-maker. She was not particularly glamorous. Throughout her husband's political career, she had played a vital role in his political decisions. The couple had not become known as Billary for no reason. The dozens of women who served as first lady before Hillary Clinton all had been important.

Bill Clinton takes the presidential oath of office in January 1993.

But few had been as independent and as strong-willed as Hillary Clinton.

Hillary Clinton began her job as first lady with a staff of twenty workers. There were specific duties she was supposed to attend to. The area of the White House where she and her staff worked soon became known as "Hillaryland." Her group's main purpose was to help support the president's agenda, especially with issues related to women, children, and families.[7] All were areas Hillary Clinton was familiar with and passionate about.

In the first month of his presidency, Bill Clinton found an official position for his wife when he formed a task force to discuss health care reform. The task force's goal was to make sure every American could afford to be treated for medical problems. Bill Clinton promised that would be done in one hundred days. The plan was criticized for several reasons. Most thought the deadline was far too short. How could he accomplish in a little more than three months something others had not been able to do in years? But with his wife leading the battle, the president was confident. Hillary Clinton was not paid for her work, but the decision to pick her was criticized anyway. One group even unsuccessfully sued the task force. The group said it was illegal for the president's wife to be in charge. In the end, the task force did not meet its hundred-day deadline. Hillary Clinton said, "I have never seen an issue that is as complicated as this. I can see why

Bill and Hillary Clinton dance together at the presidential inaugural ball in January 1993.

for fifty years people have tiptoed toward this problem and turned around and ran away."[8]

In the midst of it all, Hillary Clinton's father had a stroke. Hillary and Chelsea flew to Arkansas, where Hugh and Dorothy Rodham had moved, to be with him in the hospital. Soon after, Hugh Rodham died. His sad daughter wrote, "I couldn't help but think how my relationship with my father had evolved over time. I adored him as a little girl. . . . but I was overwhelmed with sadness for what he would now be missing. . . . I was thankful for the life, opportunities and dreams he passed along to me."[9] Today, Dorothy Rodham is almost ninety years old and lives with her daughter and son-in-law.

Losing her father was tough on Hillary. And more stress was on its way. The Clintons were about to be confronted by some major distractions that would threaten Bill Clinton's presidency and place the couple's marriage in jeopardy.

The first of several big controversies of Bill Clinton's presidency occurred in the spring of 1993. It began when he fired the staff of the White House Travel Office after problems were discovered with the office's financial records. Hillary Clinton said she had issues with the way the office was being run. She said, "There was petty cash left lying around. Cash ended up in the personal account of one of the workers. . . . that money belongs to people and it should be handled appropriately if it is in any way connected with the White House."[10]

The situation was no big deal until it was revealed that Bill Clinton's cousin was placed in charge of the travel office. Then, many thought the firings were done so a relative of the president could be put in charge. Hillary Clinton was accused of being the one who said the staff should be fired. The media came up with a name for the scandal: "Travelgate." After an investigation, the Clintons were found to have done nothing illegal. However, many still believe Hillary Clinton demanded the firings. Hillary downplayed her involvement. She said, "I expressed my concern . . . that if there were fiscal mismanagement in the Travel Office . . . it should be addressed promptly."[11]

Another controversy the Clintons were involved with was called Whitewater. That issue's long story began in the 1970s, when the Clintons and a friend bought some land in Arkansas. Their plan was to divide the property and sell each piece to make money. Years later, the business partner got into legal trouble and the Clintons also were investigated. Some believed illegal money was used to help get people, including Bill Clinton, elected to political office. Several people were convicted of crimes following the investigation. Hillary Clinton became the first wife of a president to have to testify before a grand jury. She said, "We didn't do anything wrong. We never intended to do anything wrong."[12] Eventually, the Clintons were cleared of any wrongdoings. Vince Foster, whom Hillary had worked

Hillary with the Clinton family pets, Socks and Buddy.

with at the Rose Law Firm in Arkansas, died while the Whitewater investigation was under way. By that point, Foster was working for the president. But on July 20, 1993, Foster was found dead in a park near Washington, D.C. The death was ruled a suicide. But because he was connected to the Clintons and involved in many of their controversial dealings, including Whitewater, some claimed Foster was murdered in a cover-up. A few believed the Clintons were involved in his death and Foster and Hillary Clinton were having an affair. The Clintons deny anything of the sort happened. The Whitewater issue, and Foster's untimely death, plagued the Clintons for years.

The second year of Bill Clinton's presidency did not begin well, either. First, his mother died in January. Then, in May, a woman named Paula Jones sued the president for sexual harassment. Jones once had worked for the State of Arkansas. She claimed Clinton had made sexual advances toward her when he was that state's governor. A judge dismissed the case, saying there was not enough evidence. Jones felt there was and appealed the ruling. During the appeal process, Bill Clinton decided to settle the case out of court to avoid an embarrassing trial. Jones was paid close to one million dollars to drop her charges. Bill Clinton, however, never admitted he did anything wrong.

The president was not only having personal problems. He also was having political problems. Every two

Hillary Clinton delivers a speech detailing her health care plan proposal.

years, elections are held for all seats in the House of Representatives and for many seats in the Senate. When Clinton was elected, Democrats held the majority of seats in each of those branches of government. As president, it is a huge benefit to have your political party in control of Congress. But, in the 1994 midterm elections, Republicans took control of both houses of Congress for the first time in forty years. This took a lot of power away from Clinton's presidency.

Meanwhile, Hillary Clinton was spending a lot of time defending herself and her husband. She also spent some of her time in 1995 and 1996 writing a book. It was called *It Takes a Village and Other Lessons Children*

Teach Us. The book's subject was one that had been important to her for a long time: raising children properly. She said, "What I would hope would come from this book is really a national discussion about what we [parents and society in general] can do better."[13] She accomplished that goal. When it was released in 1996, *It Takes a Village* sold extremely well. The author set off on a cross-country tour, where she met with and signed books for thousands of people. The audio version of the book even won a Grammy Award for Best Spoken Word Album in 1997. During that time period, Hillary Clinton also helped secure funding for cancer research.

Both Whitewater and the Paula Jones case were unresolved in 1996, the year Bill Clinton decided he would run for a second term. Though the controversial aspects of Clinton's presidency had dominated the news, there were many positives that took place during his first term. He had signed a popular bill that allowed workers to take paid time off to care for a sick family member. He had signed a bill that required people to wait five days before being able to buy a handgun. The president also had adopted a policy that allowed some gays and lesbians to serve in the armed forces. The policy was called "don't ask, don't tell."

For those and other reasons, Clinton remained a popular president with the American people. In this way, his presidency was similar to his governorship. People

Hillary Clinton signs copies of her book, *It Takes a Village*.

had issues with the way he handled his personal life, but they loved the way he did his job.

The Republicans nominated Bob Dole, a United States senator from Kansas, as their candidate to run against Clinton. Ross Perot also entered this race. When the votes were counted, Clinton easily had defeated both men. Again, he did not receive a majority of the popular vote. Only forty-nine percent of Americans voted for him. But it did not matter. Bill Clinton would be president of the United States for another four years. Al Gore remained by Clinton's side as vice president.

Shortly after Clinton began his second term as president, the White House had one less person living in it. In the fall of 1997, seventeen-year-old Chelsea left for college. She had chosen to attend Stanford University in Northern California. The school's campus was nearly three thousand miles from Washington, D.C. Having her daughter that far away was tough on Hillary Clinton. She had hoped Chelsea would pick a school closer to home. When Chelsea announced she wanted to go to Stanford, Hillary said, "What! Stanford is too far away! You can't go that far away! That's all the way over on the West Coast—three time zones away. We'd never get to see you."[14]

By the time Chelsea moved out of the White House, Hillary Clinton's role as first lady had changed. She continued to work on health care issues and her longtime passion of children's issues. But she was no longer her husband's main health care reform adviser. Instead, she took on several other tasks. She became a spokesperson for the United States by traveling to other countries. On trips to Africa, Asia, Europe, Latin America, and more, Hillary Clinton spoke out for human rights, health care, and education. In addition to that work, she also played the more-traditional first lady roles. That meant entertaining guests at the White House for dinners, parties, and other get-togethers.

As the controversy over the Whitewater scandal finally faded from the Clintons's lives, another emerged. The head of the Whitewater investigation, Kenneth Starr, announced he had discovered the president lied while giving testimony during the Paula Jones sexual harassment case. When he was asked, the president had said he did not have an affair with a White House intern named Monica Lewinsky. Starr believed President Clinton had. He also believed the president had asked Lewinsky to deny the affair if she was asked. If Starr's arguments proved true, President Clinton would be in deep trouble. Lying and asking someone else to lie could lead to impeachment and potential removal from office. First, though, he would need to be proven guilty of these crimes.

When Hillary Clinton heard about the accusations, she did not believe they were true. Bill Clinton told her he had talked to Lewinsky a few times. He said he had helped her try to find a job. Hillary believed her husband. They had been through plenty of scandals in their lifetimes, some similar to this one. She had no reason to believe this time was any different. She thought it was just another story made up by people who were out to get her husband.

As with most everything concerning the Clintons—especially controversial issues—the media reported the story nonstop. When asked by reporters what she thought about the accusations, Hillary Clinton said, "Certainly I believe they are false. Absolutely."[15] For his

Monica Lewinsky walks past a television cameraman as she leaves a Washington, D.C. restaurant on February 21, 1998. This was her first appearance in public after her secret claims to an affair with President Clinton.

part, Bill Clinton stuck to his story. In January 1998, he addressed the country on national television. The angry president said, "I want to say one thing to the American people. I want you to listen to me. I'm going to say this again. I did not have sexual relations with that woman, Miss Lewinsky."[16] Shaking his finger at the camera, the president continued, "I never told anybody to lie, not a single time—never. These allegations are false and I need to go back to work for the American people."[17]

Bill Clinton's story changed a few months later. On August 15, he woke Hillary and told her it had all been true. He did have an affair with Lewinsky. Hillary was stunned. She said, "What do you mean? What are you saying? Why did you lie to me?"[18] Hillary said her husband cried when she told him he had to tell Chelsea. Bill Clinton also had lied to his daughter when he told her the affair did not happen.[19]

Two days later, the president gave testimony to a grand jury. Later that night, he went back on national television. This time, he admitted to having an affair with Lewinsky. The president said, "Indeed, I did have a relationship with Miss Lewinsky that was not appropriate. In fact, it was wrong."[20] He said he never asked anyone to lie. Again, he asked the country to stop prying into his private life and let him move on with the important issues.

It was not necessarily guilt that made Clinton confess. Three weeks before his televised speech, Lewinsky had given attorneys a key piece of physical evidence. The evidence offered proof the affair took place. Many believe the president had learned about the evidence and would never have admitted to the affair if he knew he would not have been caught.

Public opinion was divided on how Hillary Clinton handled herself after finding out her husband had cheated on her and lied, especially after she decided not to get a divorce. Many said she was not holding true to what she said she believed in. She had been so outspoken over the years on women's rights and issues. But many thought that instead of the strong, empowered woman she had always been, she was being weak by allowing her husband to get away with his actions. Others thought she was showing real dedication and doing the right thing by standing by her husband through thick and thin. Still others, like Hillary herself, thought what happened between a husband and wife was a personal matter. Deciding whether or not to stay with her husband was not an easy decision for her to make. She sought the advice of many others and spent weeks thinking about it. Eventually, she chose to stay with her husband and work on the problems they were having with their marriage.

Opinion on how Bill Clinton should be punished for lying was split along party lines. Republicans thought he should be impeached. Democrats thought he should be reprimanded but not impeached. A majority of

Americans agreed with the Democrats. On December 19, 1998, the verdict finally came. The House of Representatives impeached the president for perjury, or telling a lie under oath, and obstruction of justice. Bill Clinton joined Andrew Johnson as the only presidents ever to be impeached. Johnson was impeached in 1868 for removing a member of his cabinet. That was a violation of a controversial law. The United States Supreme Court later declared the law unconstitutional.

Impeachment was only the first step to removing Clinton from office. The Senate still had to vote to remove him. A trial was held to determine whether or not to do so. In February 1999, after twenty-one days of

Hillary Clinton speaks to the men and women of Aviano Air Base, Italy, in March 1996. Standing behind her is her daughter, Chelsea, along with the First Lady of Italy, Mrs. Donatella Zingone Dini, and her daughter.

debate, the Senate found Clinton not guilty. He was impeached but could remain president.

For months, the public and media had been fixated on whether or not their president had had an affair and lied about it. Somehow, through it all, Bill Clinton kept his focus on running the country. One of his biggest achievements during his second term was helping reform the country's welfare system to help get more unemployed people working again.

As her husband's tumultuous final term as president wound down, Hillary Clinton began gearing up for a race of her own. After months of consideration and encouraging pressure from fellow Democrats, Clinton announced she would move to New York and run for a seat in the United States Senate. In doing so, she became the first former first lady to run for political office. The Clintons bought a house in Chappaqua, New York. After moving, Hillary began her campaign and won her party's nomination for the seat.

Hillary's race, like much of the Clintons's lives, was filled with difficulties. Her Republican opponent was a congressman named Rick Lazio. All along, most people thought her opponent would be Rudy Giuliani, the popular mayor of New York City. But health problems and personal issues prevented Giuliani from running, so Lazio stepped in. The Republican candidate attacked Clinton, saying she did not know anything about New

York State or its citizens. Lazio said she only moved there to enter the senate race.

One of the most controversial moments of the senate campaign had nothing to do with politics. It came when the New York Yankees visited the White House to honor their World Series victory. The team's manager gave Hillary a Yankees cap and she put it on. Since her youthful days as a tomboy in Illinois, Clinton had been a Chicago Cubs fan. Now, she was wearing a New York Yankees cap. Many took that as a sign that Clinton was willing to do whatever it took to get elected, even if it meant pretending to like something she did not. Clinton had her own explanation for wearing the cap. She told an interviewer, "I am a Cubs fan . . . [but] as a young girl I became very interested [in] and enamored of the Yankees."[21] The teams were in two different leagues, she explained, so she rooted for them both.

Clinton's ideas to revitalize the state of New York eventually won over voters. On November 7, 2000, she easily defeated Lazio. On January 3, 2001, she took office as a United States senator from New York. A little more than two weeks later, her husband completed his second and final term as president of the United States. The couple's roles had shifted: Hillary no longer was a first lady. She was the elected official. It was Bill's turn to support his wife's political career.

8
ANOTHER SHOT AT HISTORY

A familiar name replaced President Bill Clinton in the White House—the son of the person he had beaten to become president. George W. Bush, son of former president George H. W. Bush, was elected the forty-third President of the United States. The younger Bush had defeated President Clinton's vice president, Al Gore, in a close and highly controversial election. Clinton could not run again because the 22nd Amendment of the United States Constitution says a president can only be elected to two terms.

Because United States senators work in Washington, D.C., Hillary Clinton needed a place to live there in addition to her home in New York. So she and Bill bought a house there for her to live in while working in the Senate. Her new job was to represent the people of New York. Part

The Senate

The Senate is one of two branches of the United States Congress. The other is the House of Representatives. The Senate has one hundred members, two from each of the fifty states. The House of Representatives has four hundred thirty-five members, because each state receives a certain number of representatives based on its population. Members of both branches work in Washington, D.C., as representatives of the people of their state. Both the House of Representatives and Senate write and vote on bills. If a bill passes both branches, it moves to the president to be signed into law. The president can also veto a bill, stopping it from becoming law. That is, unless Congress votes to override the veto.

of her responsibility was writing and voting on bills. Senators decide whether to vote for or against every bill that comes before Congress. All bills must pass the Senate and the House of Representatives before they can go to the president to be signed into law. Senators can also write their own bills. Then, they work to get the other senators to vote their bills into law. Hillary Clinton went right to work doing that. She introduced bills that would help the people who elected her. Because she was a former first lady, Clinton was by far the best known of all the senators, but since it was her first term, she did not have a lot of power. She sat on the Environment and Public Works Committee; the Health, Labor, and Pensions Committee; and the Armed Services Committee.

Chelsea Clinton graduated from Stanford University the same year her mother took office. She then moved to England to study international relations at Oxford University. Her father had also studied there. As daughter of a former president, and now of a well-known senator, Chelsea reluctantly remained in the public eye. Her long-term relationship with Ian Klaus, whom she met at Oxford, attracted attention from the media. So did the couple's 2005 breakup. Today, Chelsea lives in New York City, where she works for a firm called Avenue Capital. She has a boyfriend named Marc Mezvinsky. Mezvinsky's father and mother are both former members of Congress. Although her mother and father are two of the most famous people in the world, Chelsea somehow manages to avoid a lot of the limelight. It is the way she and her parents have always wanted it to be.

Hillary Clinton's transition from first lady to senator began smoothly. New York was prospering. Clinton was learning the ropes of her new job. Everything was going well. But, one late-summer morning, much changed for New York, the United States, and the rest of the world.

On September 11, 2001, terrorists hijacked four planes loaded with fuel and passengers. They overpowered the pilots, took control of the planes, and crashed one of them into each of the two World Trade Center towers in New York City. The third plane crashed into the Pentagon, the United States's military headquarters, near Washington, D.C. Many believe the last plane was also headed for Washington, D.C., but instead it crashed into a field in Pennsylvania. Everyone aboard all four planes was killed. Hundreds of people in the two New York City towers (Twin Towers) and the Pentagon were

Hillary Clinton with Congressman Eliot Engel (left) and Speaker Sheldon Silver (right) at the New York State Democratic Convention on May 16, 2000.

also killed. Both Twin Towers collapsed from the damage they suffered, as did a nearby building.

In all, nearly three thousand people died. They were innocent civilians, including firefighters, police officers, and other emergency workers. Fear and panic filled the country. What would be the next target? Who had done this? Why would anyone want to kill so many innocent people? It was soon discovered that a terrorist organization named al-Qaeda was responsible. That discovery did little to ease people's minds and did nothing to fix the damage that had been done. New York City looked like an enemy had bombed it. In truth, it had.

Like most Americans, Hillary Clinton watched on television as the tragedy unfolded. In the days and months following the deadliest attack ever in the United States, Senator Clinton sought funding to help her new state rebuild. She and New York's other senator, Charles Schumer, met with President Bush to ask him for more money than he had pledged to give their state. The Republican president immediately said "yes."[1] Clinton said she became teary-eyed at his decision.[2] Later, she said how pleased she was that the country was not worried about whether someone was a Republican or Democrat when it came to this situation. She even teamed with political rivals to accomplish the task. In particular, she was happy she and New York Mayor Rudy Giuliani were able to work together to help the country. She told one newspaper, "We're all New Yorkers now. I think we were all victimized by this. There couldn't have been a city anywhere in the world that responded with more grit, resolve and just plain guts as New York did. That makes me proud every time I go and speak about it."[3]

Clinton's post-9/11 (a shortened term used to represent the date of the attacks, pronounced *nine-eleven*) efforts helped businesses and the families of victims recover. She even attended the funerals of some victims to offer her condolences.

Shortly after 9/11, the United States retaliated against its attackers. President Bush declared a war on terror. In October, the United States, England, and several other countries joined forces to go to Afghanistan. Their goal was to remove the responsible terrorist group, al-Qaeda, from power and capture its leader, Osama Bin Laden. Bin Laden has never been found.

In 2003, the United States invaded the Middle Eastern country of Iraq, after President Bush said there was evidence that country was building "weapons of mass destruction." Those weapons, he said, could be used to stage another terrorist attack on the United States or elsewhere. Weapons of mass destruction include nuclear and chemical weapons that could kill large numbers of people.

Given the president's reasoning, Senator Clinton voted to wage war on Iraq. At the end of 2003, Iraq's president, Saddam Hussein, was captured. He was put on trial for previous war crimes and executed in 2006. But the United States military never found any weapons of mass destruction. This caused a large number of Americans, including Hillary Clinton, to believe the war was not a good idea, after all.

Senator Clinton and many others also began to disagree with the way the war was being handled. Soon, Clinton began to speak out against the war. In 2007, she led a charge to call another vote on whether the war should continue and if the president should have to get the consent of Congress to continue. She said, "If the president will not bring himself to accept reality, it is time for Congress to bring reality to him."[4] No such vote has taken place.

Clinton's rivals attacked and accused her of only doing what she thought was best for her political career. They said that when waging war was popular, Clinton was for it. When it was no longer popular, she was against it. She, of course, said that was not true.

After he left office, Bill Clinton continued to travel the country and world, fighting for issues he believed in. Most

Senator Clinton speaks with U.S. Army Lt. Gen. Ray Odierno outside of Al Faw Palace in Camp Victory, Iraq, in January 2007. Clinton was in Iraq as part of a congressional delegation.

famously, he worked with the person he defeated in the 1992 presidential race, George H. W. Bush. The two teamed to help victims of two devastating natural disasters. The first was the Indian Ocean Earthquake that struck the day after Christmas 2004. It and the subsequent tsunami, or giant ocean wave, killed more than two hundred thousand people. In 2006, Clinton and Bush worked together to help after Hurricane Katrina brought catastrophic floods to the southern United States. Close to two thousand people died when the city of New Orleans, Louisiana, flooded.

Bill Clinton also wrote a book of nearly one thousand pages called *My Life*. It detailed his life from his birth in Hope, Arkansas, through his presidency and beyond. He even addressed the more controversial issues he went through. The book was a bestseller when it was released in 2004. But biography writing is one area in which Hillary beat her husband to the punch. Her autobiography, *Living History*, came out a year before her husband's. It also was a bestseller. The story told in Hillary Clinton's book paints the picture of a life similar in many ways to the life of former first lady Eleanor Roosevelt. Both women were active in helping their husbands succeed as president. Both dealt with marriages that were, at times, considered troubled. Both women also continued living public lives after their days as first lady were over.

In 2006, Hillary Clinton was re-elected to the

Senate, overwhelming her Republican opponent, John Spencer. She gained 67 percent of the votes. The next year, she did something many had long believed she would. She announced she was going to run for president of the United States. Immediately, she built a team of assistants and began campaigning for the Democratic Party's nomination. Her closest competitor in early polls was Illinois Senator Barack Obama. Obama emerged as a popular figure, due in part to his charisma and popular books.

As the candidates debated and campaigned, Hillary Clinton became the early

Senator and presidential candidate Hillary Clinton speaks at the Joseph Caleb Center in Miami on February 20, 2007.

front-runner. Powerful politicians and financial donors began to pledge support to her campaign. A poll conducted in August 2007 showed 49 percent of voters in the state of California said they planned to vote for Clinton in the Democratic primary.[5] Only 19 percent said they would vote for Obama.[6] Results generally are closer in national polls. But, even in those, Hillary Clinton leads nearly every time.

The Democratic Party's nomination will be decided in August 2008. The Republican candidate will be chosen a week later. Then, in November, the country will choose its next president from those two, and from candidates that are running for less-popular political parties.

If Hillary Clinton is elected president of the United States, it will be a historic moment. No woman has ever been president. As much as women's status in society has risen, there still are many who are not comfortable with a woman president. Not surprisingly, women support Clinton more strongly than men do, one 2007 poll showed.[7] The same poll showed Obama was supported equally by both women and men.[8] Clinton knows she is fighting that gender bias. She said, "I'm proud to be running to be the first woman president, but I'm not running because I'm a woman. I'm running because I think I'm the best qualified and experienced to hit the ground running and get the job done."[9]

Many people would not be surprised if she wins. At least one person saw the possibility as far back as the spring of 1969, when a strong-willed young woman from a small town in Illinois delivered an inspirational graduation speech. When she finished, a classmate turned to her mother and said, "Take a good look at her. She will probably be the president of the United States someday."[10] Since that moment nearly forty years ago, Hillary Rodham Clinton has continued making history. If she has her way, she will prove that classmate right.

CHRONOLOGY

1947   Hillary Diane Rodham born on October 26, in Chicago, Illinois, to Hugh and Dorothy Rodham. Lives with family in one-bedroom apartment.

1950   Moves with family to Chicago suburb of Park Ridge, Illinois; father commutes to Chicago for work, mother stays at home to take care of family; brother, Hugh Rodham, born.

1954   Brother, Anthony Rodham, born.

1960   Helps Republicans investigate voter addresses after Democrat John F. Kennedy wins presidency; gets first summer job working for the Park Ridge Park District.

1961   Writes letter to NASA saying she would like to be an astronaut; NASA responds by saying females are not accepted into its space program.

1963   Hears speech given by civil rights activist Dr. Martin Luther King, Jr., in Chicago.

1964   Joins Young Republicans; campaigns for Barry Goldwater in his run for the presidency.

1965   Moves to Wellesley, Massachusetts, to begin freshman year at Wellesley College, an all-female school; initially struggles to adapt; elected president of Young Republicans.

1966   Resigns Young Republicans post; becomes Democrat.

1968   Campaigns for Eugene McCarthy, who is seeking the Democratic Party's nomination for president; interns in Washington, D.C., for a Republican congressman; attends Republican National Convention in Miami to help Nelson Rockefeller gain the Republican presidential nomination; attends Democratic National Convention in Chicago; elected president of Wellesley's senior class.

1969   Becomes first-ever student graduation speaker at Wellesley; upstages a U.S. senator with speech and gains nationally notoriety for doing so; graduates from Wellesley; moves to New Haven, Connecticut, to attend Yale Law School.

1970   Meets Marian Wright Edelman; interns with Edelman working on children's issues in Washington, D.C.; meets fellow law school student, Bill Clinton.

1971   Begins dating Bill Clinton; moves into apartment with Clinton.

1972   Moves with Bill Clinton to Texas for summer to work on Democrat George McGovern's presidential campaign; spends a fourth year at Yale Law School working on children's issues

1973   Graduates, with Bill Clinton, from Yale Law School; rejects Clinton's marriage proposal; moves to Massachusetts to work as attorney for the Children's Defense Fund.

1974	Moves to Washington, D.C., to work on impeachment case against President Richard Nixon; takes teaching job at University of Arkansas; helps Clinton run for U.S. House of Representatives.
1975	Marries Bill Clinton on October 11.
1976	Helps Bill Clinton get elected as attorney general of Arkansas; moves to Little Rock; begins work for Rose Law Firm.
1979	Becomes first lady of Arkansas when Bill Clinton is elected state governor.
1980	Gives birth to Chelsea Victoria Clinton on February 27; husband loses re-election bid.
1982	Decides to change name from Hillary Rodham to Hillary Rodham Clinton; husband wins election and again serves as Arkansas governor.
1983	Leads Arkansas Education Standards Committee.
1984	Named Arkansas Woman of the Year by a newspaper.
1992	Responds publicly to allegations of husband's womanizing; helps husband get elected forty-second President of the United States.
1993	Moves with family into White House; becomes America's first lady; heads national health care reform task force; father dies on April 7; Whitewater controversy surfaces; gets wrapped up in Travelgate controversy.

1996   Publishes *It Takes a Village and Other Lessons Children Teach Us*; embarks on cross-country book tour.

1997   *It Takes a Village* wins Grammy Award for Best Spoken Word Album; begins traveling to other countries as a United States spokesperson.

1998   Husband admits to an affair with White House intern Monica Lewinsky; Bill Clinton impeached.

2000   Moves to New York; elected to United States Senate.

2001   Nearly three thousand people die when hijacked planes crash into the World Trade Center towers in New York City, the Pentagon in Washington, D.C., and a field in Pennsylvania; secures additional funding to help state's recovery.

2002   Votes to allow president to wage war on Iraq.

2003   Publishes autobiography, *Living History*.

2006   Reelected to Senate.

2007   Announces decision to run for president in 2008.

CHAPTER NOTES

Chapter 1. A Historic Speech

1. Hillary Rodham Clinton, *Living History* (New York: Scribner, 2003), p. 39.

2. Wellesley College 1969 Student Commencement Speech, July 19, 1999, <http://www.wellesley.edu/ PublicAffairs/Commencement/1969/053169hillary.html> (March 27, 2007).

3. Wellesley College Commencement Address 1969 Senator Edward W. Brooke, July 15, 1999, <http://www. wellesley.edu/PublicAffairs/Commencement/1969/brooke. html> (March 27, 2007).

4. Ibid.

5. Ibid.

6. Donnie Radcliffe, *A First Lady for Our Time* (New York: Warner Books, 1993), p. 81.

7. Wellesley College 1969 Student Commencement Speech, July 19, 1999, <http://www.wellesley.edu/ PublicAffairs/Commencement/1969/053169hillary.html> (May 10, 2007).

8. Radcliffe, p. 81.

9. Wellesley College 1969 Student Commencement Speech, July 19, 1999, <http://www.wellesley.edu/ PublicAffairs/Commencement/1969/053169hillary.html> (May 10, 2007).

10. Ibid.

11. Ibid.

12. *Frontline: Hillary's Class*, 60-minute-long program, *PBS.org*, n.d., <http://www.pbs.org/wgbh/pages/frontline/ twenty/watch/hillary.html> (May 14, 2007).

13. Ibid.

14. Ibid.

Chapter 2. Young Republican

1. Howard B. Furer, *Chicago: A Chronological and Documentary History* (Dobbs Ferry, New York: Oceana Publications, 1974), p. 19.

2. "1833 Incorporated as a Town—Origin of Name," *Chicago Timeline*, The Chicago Public Library, August 1997, <http://www.chipublib.org/004chicago/timeline/originame. html> (March 15, 2007).

3. Furer, p. 33.

4. "Population of Chicago by Decades 1830–2000," *Chicago Timeline*, The Chicago Public Library, April 2001, <http://www.chipublib.org/004chicago/timeline/population. html> (March 30, 2007).

5. Hillary Rodham Clinton, *Living History* (New York: Scribner, 2003), p. 9.

6. "Growing Up in Illinois," *Hillaryclinton.com*, n.d., <http://www.hillaryclinton.com/about/growingup/> (April 1, 2007).

7. Hillary Rodham Clinton, *It Takes a Village and Other Lessons Children Teach Us* (New York: Simon and Schuster, 1996), p. 23.

8. Ibid., p. 22.

9. Ibid.

10. Claire G. Osborne, ed., *Hillary Rodham Clinton: A Portrait in Her Own Words* (New York: Avon Books, 1997), p. 3.

11. Ibid.

12. Clinton, *It Takes a Village and Other Lessons Children Teach Us*, p. 22.

13. Ibid.

14. Clinton, *Living History*, p. 17.

15. Ibid.

16. Ibid., p. 12.

17. The Associated Press, "Women's Hall of Fame Honors Hillary Clinton, 9 Others," *USA Today*, October 9, 2005, <http://www.usatoday.com/news/washington/2005-10-09-women-clinton_x.htm> (April 17, 2007).

18. Clinton, *It Takes a Village and Other Lessons Children Teach Us*, p. 27.

19. "Civil Rights: On the 42nd Anniversary of Bloody Sunday in Selma," Hillary for President, <http://www.hillaryclinton.com/news/speech/view/?id=1362> (March 30, 2007).

20. Clinton, *Living History*, p. 21.

21. Osborne, p. 8.

22. Clinton, *Living History*, p. 25.

Chapter 3. Speaking Out

1. Claire G. Osborne, ed., *Hillary Rodham Clinton: A Portrait in Her Own Words* (New York: Avon Books, 1997), p. 9.

2. Donnie Radcliffe, *A First Lady for Our Time* (New York: Warner Books, 1993), p. 57.

3. Hillary Rodham Clinton, *Living History* (New York: Scribner, 2003), p. 27.

4. Ibid., p. 31.

5. David L. Anderson, *The Columbia Guide to the Vietnam War* (New York: Columbia University Press, 2002), p. 78.

6. Ibid.

7. Clinton, *Living History*, p. 31.

8. Radcliffe, p. 73.

9. Joyce Milton, *The First Partner: Hillary Rodham Clinton* (New York: Perennial, 2000), p. 31

10. Clinton, *Living History*, p. 37.

11. Radcliffe, pp. 74–75.

12. Osborne, p. 10.

13. Radcliffe, p. 80.

14. Clinton, *Living History*, p. 40.

15. Radcliffe, p. 82.

16. Clinton, *Living History*, p. 42.

17. Ibid., p. 43.

Chapter 4. Two Law Students

1. Hillary Rodham Clinton, *Living History* (New York: Scribner, 2003), pp. 45–46.

2. Claire G. Osborne, ed., *Hillary Rodham Clinton: A Portrait in Her Own Words* (New York: Avon Books, 1997), p. 14.

3. Bill Clinton, *My Life* (New York: Alfred A. Knopf, 2004), p. 181.

4. Ibid., p. 182.

5. Ibid., p. 20.

6. Clinton, *Living History*, p. 61.

7. Ibid., p. 64.

8. Ibid., p. 70.

9. Bill Clinton, *My Life*, p. 233.

10. Joyce Milton, *The First Partner: Hillary Rodham Clinton* (New York: Perennial, 2000), p. 102.

11. Clinton, *Living History*, p. 81.

Chapter 5. First Lady of Arkansas

1. Hillary Rodham Clinton, *Living History* (New York: Scribner, 2003), p. 91.

2. Ibid.

3. Claire G. Osborne, ed., *Hillary Rodham Clinton: A Portrait in Her Own Words* (New York: Avon Books, 1997), pp. 20–21.

4. Osborne, p. 51.

5. Ibid., p. 72

6. Bill Clinton, "Announcement Speech," October 3, 1991, *4president.org*, <http://www.4president.org/speeches/billclinton1992announcement.htm> (May 14, 2007).

7. Osborne, p. 37.

Chapter 6. Presidential Campaign

1. Hillary Rodham Clinton, *Living History* (New York: Scribner, 2003), p. 98.

2. Claire G. Osborne, ed., *Hillary Rodham Clinton: A Portrait in Her Own Words* (New York: Avon Books, 1997), p. 52

3. Ibid.

4. Joyce Milton, *The First Partner: Hillary Rodham Clinton* (New York: Perennial, 2000), p. 220.

5. Ibid., p. 221.

6. Osborne, p. 47.

7. Clinton, *Living History*, p. 113.

8. Ibid., p. 117.

9. Ibid., p. 119.

Chapter 7. A Busy First Lady

1. Bill Clinton's First Inaugural Address, January 21, 1993, *Bartleby.com*, <http://www.bartleby.com/124/pres64. html> (April 23, 2007).

2. Hillary Rodham Clinton, *Living History* (New York: Scribner, 2003), p. 125.

3. Claire G. Osborne, ed., *Hillary Rodham Clinton: A Portrait in Her Own Words* (New York: Avon Books, 1997), p. 129.

4. "White House Facts," The White House official Web site, n.d., <http://www.whitehouse.gov/history/facts.html> (May 15, 2007).

5. Arden Davis Melick, *Wives of the Presidents* (Maplewood, N. J.: Hammond, 1977), p. 78.

6. Ibid., p. 80.

7. Clinton, *Living History*, p. 132.

8. Osborne, p. 148.

9. Clinton, *Living History*, pp. 163–164.

10. Osborne, p. 133.

11. Ibid.

12. Osborne, p. 138.

13. Ibid., p. 172.

14. Clinton, *Living History*, p. 341.

15. James Bennet, "The President Under Fire: The First Lady; Rallying the Defense of Her Husband, Again," *The New York Times*, January 25, 1998, <http://query.nytimes.com/gst/fullpage.html?res=9B07E5DC133BF936A15752C0A96E958260> (May 9, 2007).

16. "Grand Jury Convenes Without Lewinsky Testimony: Mrs. Clinton Says Attack Is a 'Right-wing Conspiracy,' " *CNN.com*, January 27, 1998, <http://www.cnn.com/ALLPOLITICS/1998/01/27/clinton.main/> (May 10, 2007).

17. Ibid.

18. Clinton, Living History, p. 466.

19. Ibid.

20. President Bill Clinton: August 17, 1998 speech, *CNN.com*, <http://www.cnn.com/ALLPOLITICS/1998/08/17/speech/transcript.html> (May 4, 2007).

21. Joyce Milton, *The First Partner: Hillary Rodham Clinton*, softcover edition (New York: Perennial, 2000), p. 415.

Chapter 8. Another Shot at History

1. David Barstow, "A Nation Challenged: Federal Aid; Old Rivals, but One Voice in Request for Help," *The New York Times*, September 19, 2001, <http://query.nytimes.com/gst/fullpage.html?res=9E0CE3D9123BF93AA2575AC0A9679C8B63&sec=&spon=&pagewanted=1> (May 9, 2007).

2. Ibid.

3. Jennifer Steinhauer and Raymond Hernandez, "A Nation Challenged: The Mayor; Giuliani and Senator Clinton: Once Rivals, Now Allies," *The New York Times*, September 22, 2001, <http://query.nytimes.com/gst/fullpage.html?res=9800E7DC163AF931A1575AC0A9679C8B63&sec=&spon=&pagewanted=2> (May 9, 2007).

4. Devlin Barrett, "Clinton Seeks New Vote in Authorizing Military Effort in Iraq," The Associated Press, printed on May 3, 2007, at *Newsday.com*, <http://www.newsday.com/news/local/wire/newyork/ny-bc-ny—clinton-iraq0503may03,0, 6761950.story?coll=ny-region-apnewyork> (May 10, 2007).

5. The Associated Press, "Poll: Nearly Half Favoring Clinton in Calif. Democratic Primary," *The San Jose Mercury News,* August 17, 2007, <http://www.mercurynews.com/breakingnews/ci_6648360> (August 22, 2007).

6. Ibid.

7. Matt Stearns, "Will U.S. Voters Elect a Woman as President?" *McClatchy Newspapers,* August 21, 2007, <http://seattletimes.nwsource.com/html/nationworld/2003845865_clinton21.html> (August 22, 2007).

8. Ibid.

9. Ibid.

10. *Frontline: Hillary's Class,* 60-minute-long program, *PBS.org,* n.d., <http://www.pbs.org/wgbh/pages/frontline/twenty/watch/hillary.html>, (May 24, 2007).

FURTHER READING

Books by Hillary Rodham Clinton

Clinton, Hillary Rodham. *It Takes a Village: And Other Lessons Children Teach Us.* New York: Simon and Schuster, 1996.

Clinton, Hillary Rodham. *Living History.* New York: Simon & Schuster, 2003.

Clinton, Hillary Rodham, and Claire G. Osborne. *The Unique Voice of Hillary Rodham Clinton: A Portrait in Her Own Words.* New York: Avon Books, 1997.

Books

Burgan, Michael. *Hillary Rodham Clinton.* New York: Compass Point Books, 2005.

Freedman, Jeri. *Hillary Rodham Clinton: Profile of a Leading Democrat.* Washington, D.C.: Rosen Publishing Group, 2007.

Guernsey, Joann Bren. *Hillary Rodham Clinton.* New York: First Avenue Editions, 2005.

Internet Addresses

Hillary for President
<http://hillaryclinton.com>

New York Senator Hillary Rodham Clinton
<http://www.clinton.senate.gov>

White House Biography of First Lady Hillary Clinton
<http://www.whitehouse.gov/history/firstladies/hc42.html>

Hillary Clinton's Senate Voting Record
<http://projects.washingtonpost.com/congress/members/c001041/>

INDEX